COLLINS AURA GARDEN

GW00336578

COLOURFUL SHRUBS

KENNETH A. BECKETT

COLLINS

Products mentioned in this book

'Clean-Up'	contains	tar acids
'Picket'	contains	permethrin
ICI Slug Pellets	contains	metaldehyde
'Sybol'	contains	pirimiphos-methyl

Products marked thus '*Sybol*' are trade marks of Imperial Chemical Industries plc
Read the label before you buy: use pesticides safely.

Editor Maggie Daykin
Designers James Marks, Steve Wilson
Picture research Moira McIlroy

This edition first published 1988 by
William Collins Sons & Co Ltd
London · Glasgow · Sydney
Auckland · Toronto · Johannesburg

British Library Cataloguing in Publication Data

Beckett, Kenneth A.
 Colourful shrubs.——(Collins Aura garden handbooks).
 1. Shrubs
 I. Title
 635.9'76   SB435

ISBN 0–00–412376–X

Photoset by Bookworm Typesetting
Printed and bound in Hong Kong by Dai Nippon Printing
Company

Front cover: Pieris formosa forrestii
Back cover: Mixed shrub border
Both by the Harry Smith Horticultural Photographic Collection

CONTENTS

INTRODUCTION

No garden can ever have that mature look without shrubs. Holding their shape the year round they provide form and substance and act as a satisfying background for less permanent plantings. Furthermore, they can be colourful and attractive in their own right.

Annuals must be replaced éach year. Border perennials require cutting back annually and some also should be staked. Shrubs, being permanent, thrive without these gardening chores. Some need an annual pruning but many do not. Weeding will be necessary during the early stages, but herbicides can take care of this, being easier to use among shrubs than annuals and perennials. For these reasons shrubs are as popular, if not more so, than they have ever been.

Certainly no other plant group has so many facets of attractiveness. In habit they range from mat-formers and hummocks to tall, billowy forms, and these have as many textures as there are leaf sizes, shapes and colours. Some have a profusion of small flowers or fewer large ones in a wide range of colours which, in some cases, are fragrant also. The flowers may be followed by decorative berries or seed heads. Other shrubs have colourful stems or bark which lends them a new dimension of beauty in winter when the leaves have fallen.

So, what exactly is a shrub and how do we define it? When mature, its basic form is either a cluster of woody stems rising from below ground level or from a short, thick trunk at or just above the soil. Some shrubs get very large and it is sometimes difficult to decide whether these are shrubs or trees. For the purposes of this book a large shrub is one seldom above 3m (10ft) and taking some years to attain this size. Some have a greater potential height, but remain smaller because of customary annual pruning. For example, this applies to some buddleias, willows and dogwoods.

Whatever the size of your garden, this book will help you to choose shrubs of lasting beauty.

ABOVE The dwarf
Hebe vernicosa
produces a profusion
of blossom every
summer.
LEFT *Hebe x
franciscana*
'Variegata' highlights
a mixed planting of
dwarf shrubs.
BELOW *Pyrus
salicifolia* 'Pendula'
contrasts beautifully
with a red-flowered
rhododendron.

USES IN THE GARDEN

For effective background planting, especially in the larger garden, evergreen shrubs which rely primarily on their pleasing green foliage, such as hollies (*Ilex*), Portugal laurel (*Prunus lusitanica*), *Elaeagnus*, *Griselinia*, Lawson cypress (*Chamaecyparis lawsoniana*) and *Thuja plicata* are essential. With an all year backdrop of this sort in position, the scene is set for the colourful species and cultivated varieties (cultivars) to perform in perfect conditions. In the smaller garden every shrub must have a colourful phase at some time of the year and each one should enhance or contrast with the others. For example, even rather dull out of bloom lilacs provide a necessary background for late flowering buddleias and hydrangeas; in winter, evergreen rhododendrons, camellias or ceanothuses nicely set off the naked twigged flowers of *Viburnum farreri (fragrans)* and *Hamamelis mollis*.

If only a few colourful shrubs are to be grown in strategic sites around the garden these should be chosen with care, selecting only those with good flowers and foliage, such as camellias and mahonias, many of the rhododendrons, roses and hydrangeas.

Although colourful shrubs are usually sited for their star-performing role in the garden, they can also serve the following functions.

Screens and windbreaks Some of the taller shrubs make good screens and low windbreaks. Because of their colourful impact however, it is recommended that a variety of species and cultivars is used, with no more than say, three or four of each sort. The gold-splashed leaves of *Elaeagnus pungens* 'Maculata' and the young red ones of *Photinia* x 'Red Robin' or 'Robusta' are splendid in moderation but a row can be overpowering. Evergreens should be chosen for this purpose as they give all year wind protection and privacy. Other possibilities are variegated hollies, the yellow-fruiting *Cotoneaster* x 'Rothschildianus' or red *C.salicifolius*.

An alternative is to mix evergreens with deciduous shrubs to gain variety of effect and to add the colour of young unfolding leaves and dying autumn foliage. For example, with the above mentioned evergreens could be associated *Amelanchier* (snowy mespilus), *Euonymus europaeus* 'Red Cascade', *Neillia thibetica* (*longiracemosa*), *Stephanandra tanakae*, or *Viburnum opulus* or *betulifolium*.

Hedges Some 'of the most highly approved hedging shrubs are also beautiful in bloom. One has only to think of *Berberis darwinii, B.x stenophylla, Escallonia* and all pyracanthas, lavender, *Potentilla fruticosa* 'Friedrichsenii' or 'Vilmorinii', *Rosa rugosa* and cultivars to be assured of this.

Once again, a thought should be given to the over-powering effect that a long solid row of one type of plant can provide, especially in a small garden. Seldom seen these days, but an idea worth reviving is the mosaic hedge. This is a mixture of different coloured foliages, so chosen that together they create a very pleasing, contrasting mosaic

FAR LEFT The coppery-red young leaves of *Photinia x fraseri.*
LEFT The remarkably spiny leaves of *Ilex aquifolium* 'Ferox Argentea'.
BELOW *Osmanthus x burkwoodii* makes a good informal hedge.

patterns, with one species predominating to form a "framework". For example, copper beech or the purple-leaved cherry plum (*Prunus cerasifera* 'Pissardii') can be used in this capacity with groups or single plants of the yellow *Philadelphus coronarius* 'Aureus' or *Physocarpus opulifolius* 'Luteus' blended with the soft greens of *Lonicera tatarica*, or common hawthorn. An evergreen mixture might be *Osmanthus* (x *Osmarea*) *burkwoodii* with *Elaeagnus pungens* 'Maculata' or 'Gilt Edge' and *Viburnum tinus* 'Purpureum' or, in mild areas, the more effective *Pittosporum tenuifolium* 'Purpureum'.

There are endless possibilities for mosaic mixtures though it is wise to choose species and cultivars of fairly equal vigour.

Ground-cover Bare soil is quickly colonised by weeds and creates a gardening chore. To minimise and finally do away with this unnecessary work the planting of ground-cover has become popular.

Ground-cover plants must be low-growing and of dense habit. They should also be good to look at and if possible, downright colourful, especially as some areas chosen for ground-cover such as beneath trees and shrubs, shady corners and banks need brightening up. Nothing will more lighten a shady place than the green and gold of *Hypericum calycinum*, the vividly cream-margined foliage of *Vinca major* 'Variegata' or *Euonymus fortunei* 'Silver Queen'. For sunnier sites there are *Juniperus communis*

'Depressa Aurea', *Cotoneaster microphylla cochleatus, Hebe* 'Pagei' and various heaths (*Erica*) and heathers (*Calluna*).

Variety is the spice of life and so it is with ground-cover. No more than a few square metres should be covered with any one species. Where a shrub border or bed is to be covered, some thought should be given to the contrasting or enhancement effect with the shrubs or trees above; for example, the use of the grey-purple leaved sage (*Salvia officinalis* 'Purpurea') beneath forsythia sets off that yellow-flowered shrub most strikingly. *Vinca minor* 'Variegata' on the other hand does nothing as ground-cover to, say, the silver hedgehog holly (*Ilex aquifolium* 'Ferox Argentea').

Ground-cover plants should be juxtaposed to blend with each other. Too much contrast on the ground will detract from the plants they surround.

The hardier small-leaved and whipcord hebes provide varied-hued foliage and make a very satisfying planting of year round appeal. Hebes fare best in well-drained soils. Otherwise, they tend to be undemanding, adaptable shrubs.

Camellia x williamsii embraces a large group of vigorous, floriferous, very garden-worthy cultivars. This clear pink one, called 'Parkside', is a large, semi-double form.

Accent and specimen shrubs

While sheer impact of pigment alone may be considered enough when choosing colourful shrubs for the garden, there are further considerations. This is especially true when selecting for a prominent position, say at the end of a path or on a lawn near the house. Important accent plants of this kind must be decorative as long as possible during the year, so they need the qualities of good foliage or overall shape ideally in addition to flowers. Common lilac (*Syringa vulgaris*) is a classic example of a rather dull shrub except for the 3-4 weeks each year when it becomes smothered with fragrant blossom.

Common buddleia (*Buddleia davidii*) and its superior cultivars on the other hand, have elegantly tapered leaves, grey-white beneath, which are attractive before and during flowering. And its fragrant flowers will attract many butterflies into your garden.

There are many other fine examples of shrubs with good foliage and flowers. All the camellias and mahonias and many of the larger leaved rhododendrons are splendid. For limy soils there are several barberries, notably *Berberis darwinii*, *Rosa rugosa*, several ceanothuses, such as *C.impressus* and *thyrsiflorus*, *Clerodendrum fargesii*, *Prunus lusitanica*, and *Cytisus battandieri*. All these provide flowers and foliage with the exception of the clerodendrum and rose which also have colourful fruits.

There are several shrubs with indifferent flowers but pleasing foliage and colourful fruits, notably *Berberis jamesiana* and several smaller deciduous barberries, various spindles (*Euonymus*) and hollies (*Ilex*), all the firethorns and such deciduous viburnums as *V.betulifolium* and *V.trilobum*.

PROSTRATE SHRUBS

Flat growing or carpeting shrubs have a number of uses in the garden. As mentioned previously, the more densely habited ones are perfect for ground-cover between taller species or on banks. They are also most effective tumbling over the edge of a retaining wall. An intriguing result can be had by creating a mosaic on a flat site. If you have an over-large lawn and wish to cut down the mowing chore, one side of it could be turned over to this idea.

Evergreens On the whole, evergreen or semi-evergreen carpeting shrubs are the most useful. Not only are they the most efficient weed smotherers, but there is something to see during the winter. Rose of Sharon (*Hypericum calycinum*) and the periwinkles (*Vinca major* and *minor*) have been mentioned already and are indispensable where the soil is poor and/or dry. Japanese spurge *Pachysandra terminalis* is also a good standby, but only the 'Variegata' form can just qualify as "colourful". It does not thrive where the soil is dry. Apart from this and the variegated periwinkles there are not many carpeting shrubs with variegated leaves.

Among the heaths and heathers however, there are several cultivars with very colourful foliage. The common heather (*Calluna vulgaris*) provides the most: 'Beoley Gold' has bright golden-yellow shoots throughout the year; 'Golden Feather' is flatter growing with the foliage yellow in summer and reddish-orange in winter. 'Sir John Charrington' and 'Wickwar Flame' are orange-yellow in summer, bright red in winter. In addition to their foliage, all have showy late summer flowers.

Some of the bell heathers (*Erica cinerea*) are equally good: 'Windlebrook' has light golden-yellow leaves in summer, taking on orange-gold tints in winter; 'Rock Pool' is similar but much flatter growing.

The Cornish heath (*Erica vagans*) 'Valerie Proudley' is yellow throughout the year. Several heaths and heathers also have silvery-grey foliage, for example, *Calluna vulgaris* 'Silver Knight', 'Silver Queen' and 'Silver Rose'; *Erica tetralix* 'Alba Mollis' with its white flowers and 'Hookstone Pink'.

Flowers Evergreen foliage and winter flowers are provided in abundance by the lime tolerant winter heath, *Erica carnea*. 'Ann Sparkes' has rich purple-red flowers and orange-yellow, bronze-red-tipped foliage – an exotic mixture. 'King George' is a good old standby with deep pink blooms, and 'Pink Spangles' is lighter pink; 'Springwood Pink' is more wide spreading.

Among the most profusely blooming carpeting shrubs are the rock roses (*Helianthemum*). Larger flowers of greater substance and longer life are borne by several very low growing rhododendrons. Waxy bell-shaped scarlet bells grace *R.forrestii repens* which, even when not in bloom is well worth a second glance for its glossy deep green leaves. *R.prostratum* has tiny lustrous leaves in a close mat above which appear almost saucer-shaped blooms of purple-rose spotted with crimson. Like all rhododendrons they need a neutral to acid soil to thrive.

Blue is not a common colour in any shrub category but those available are well worth growing. *Ceanothus thyrsiflorus repens* has vigour and density of growth, handsome glossy foliage and lots of fluffy clusters of powder-blue flowers. However, there appear to be two or more forms of this Californian lilac in cultivation. All start off more or less prostrate but one sort at least eventually builds up into a mound 90-120cm (3-4ft) in height. *C.gloriosus* and *C.prostratus* are always flat mats, but not so easy to obtain.

Rosmarinus lavandulaceus (*officinalis prostratus*) is a delightful mat-forming rosemary with violet-blue flowers. Regrettably it is not as hardy as common rosemary but in a sheltered site is well worth trying. It looks most impressive curtaining a retaining wall.

LEFT *Vinca major* 'Variegata' brightens up shady corners.
TOP *Helianthemum* 'Fire Dragon' is splendid for a dry, sunny bank, where it will flower generously in summer.
ABOVE *Hypericum calycinum* with its large, golden flowers, grows in sun or shade and is almost indestructible ground cover.

The South African *Euryops acraeus (evansii)* is more likely to be seen on the rock garden or raised bed, but is well worth trying as ground-cover. Its dense hummocks of vivid grey leaves are usually studded with rich yellow daisy blooms in early summer. Also yellow but very different and much larger are the prostrate brooms, *Genista lydia* and *Cytisus* x *beanii*. Both have tiny, short lived leaves and dense sheaves of green stems which render them evergreen in appearance. The abandon with which they produce their tiny bright yellow pea flowers has to be seen to be believed.

The carpeting shrubby veronica, *Hebe (pinguifolia)* 'Pagei' produces abundant white flowers with

Hebe 'Pagei' is almost certainly a hybrid of *H. pinguifolia*. It is one of the hardiest and possibly the greyest-leaved of all the hebes. The small, white flowers appear in May. A very rewarding choice for rock gardens.

crimson-tipped stamens. Its primary value in the garden however, is the neat, blue-grey foliage. Unlike the Rose of Sharon (*Hypericum calycinum*), *H.polyphyllum* and *H.olympicum* do not spread invasively underground. Instead they form dense cushions 30-45cm (1-1½ft) wide, of small greyish leaves, and in summer become smothered with multistamened, bright yellow flowers. Although usually grown as rock plants they have wider uses around the garden. *H.p.*'Sulphureum' has lemon-yellow blooms.

Evergreen fruiters Flattest of the cotoneasters is *C.dammeri*, a vigorous plant which hugs every contour of the ground. The small dark green leaves make a nice foil for the red berries, though it is not a free fruiter. Less ground hugging but more prolific with its berries is the hybrid 'Coral Beauty'.

Rich green leaves and red berries are also the hallmark of *Gaultheria procumbens*, the berries being larger and brighter. In the peaty soil it needs, it can spread with great vigour. In its native N.America it is called wintergreen or checkerberry. The Himalayan *G.trichophylla* has fruits of a startling blue but they are not always freely borne. *Pernettya* and *Vaccinium* are the same family as *Gaultheria* (*Ericaceae* or heather family) and all need neutral to acid, preferably peaty soil. *Pernettya prostrata pentlandii* eventually rises to 30cm (1ft) but spreads more widely. It bears clusters of blue-purple fruits.

The European cowberry, *Vaccinium vitis-idaea*, returns us to the theme of rich glossy leaves and red berries. When well established it is the most reliable fruiter of them all, especially the selection called 'Koralle'; but beware birds!

When well suited *Ceratostigma plumbaginoides* forms carpets 1.2m (4ft) or more wide and bears a profusion of pure blue flowers in the early autumn. Prefers full sun and a well-drained soil.

Deciduous flowering carpeters
Although evergreens provide winter interest and are more efficient at smothering the weeds, there are several decorative deciduous species which add variety of texture and tender green spring foliage to the scene. None of the dwarf willows (*Salix*) can be described as colourful, but those that produce their catkins in late winter are welcome garden plants. *S.apoda* is completely flat with pleasing semi-glossy leaves in summer; in early spring, erect silvery catkins appear which turn yellow as the stamens expand. A sprawling shrublet to 25cm (10in) or so tall, the whortleberry-leaved willow (*Salix myrsinites*) has silvery pink-tinted catkins with the unfolding leaves. *Stephanandra incisa* 'Crispa' ('Prostrata') forms low mounds of orangy-brown stems which pick up the winter light in an attractive way. The sharply toothed leaves are fresh green and take on yellow to amber tints in autumn.

There are several low-growing cultivars of shrubby cinquefoil (*Potentilla fruticosa*). These have small, fingered leaves and a succession of flowers like small single roses. Less than 45cm (1½ft) tall are the yellow to coppery-red 'Tangerine'; the yellow, silvery leaved 'Beesii' ('Nana Argentea'), and the aptly named 'Tilford Cream'. Of similar size is *Spiraea japonica* 'Little Princess', the low mounds of small leaves thickly studded with vivid pompons of tiny rose-crimson flowers.

Fuchsias are familiar to most gardeners and some are good garden plants. 'Corallina' ('Exoniensis') produces low arching stems less than 30cm (1ft) tall, set with large, pendent, purple and crimson flowers in summer and autumn.

Pure, almost gentian blue is found in *Ceratostigma plumbaginoides*, a hardy relative of the sub-tropical plumbago. Although classed as a shrub it usually dies back to ground level and really behaves like a herbaceous perennial. In late autumn, red leaves join the blue, primrose-shaped flowers.

DWARF SHRUBS

For the purposes of this book, dwarf shrubs are like smaller versions of large ones, that is they are mostly not much wider than tall. This distinguishes them from ground-cover shrubs which are a good deal wider than tall. A maximum height range of 30-90cm (1-3ft) has been chosen, though some species may, in time exceed this by a little.

Dwarf shrubs as defined above are particularly valuable in gardens of all sizes, but most of all in small ones. They are the ideal material for filling in the front of a border or bed of larger shrubs and perfect for foundation planting at the foot of house walls. Grouped by themselves in island beds they can make a most satisfying feature, while for filling in small, awkward corners with something attractive and of permanent interest, they have no peer.

Flowers and evergreen foliage A surprising number of dwarf shrubs combine showy flowers with decorative foliage. One of the best and commonest examples is *Senecio* x 'Sunshine', a shrubby hybrid ragwort that parades in nurseries and garden centres under one or other of its parents' names, *S.greyi* and *S.laxifolius*. Its profusion of bright yellow daisy flowers contrasts most tellingly with the silvery-grey, white-backed leaves. Cotton laven-

ABOVE Perhaps the best cotton lavender, *Santolina chamaecyparissus insularis* is also known as *S. neapolitana.* RIGHT 'Sunshine' is a perfect name for this shrubby *Senecio.* TOP FAR RIGHT *Convolvulus cneorum* has leaves of silver with a satin sheen. FAR RIGHT 'Munstead' is the hardiest dwarf lavender.

der (*Santolina chamaecyparissus*) and curry plant (*Helichrysum italicum* [*angustifolium*]) also combine grey or silver foliage with yellow flowers though the leaves are very narrow and the flowers lack ray florets. Both are excellent for dry sunny places.

Abundant bright yellow pea flowers proclaim the brooms (various species of *Cytisus* and *Genista*). Among those that come into the dwarf shrub category, *Genista hispanica* is perhaps the showiest forming rounded hummocks of green prickles that are completely hidden by brilliant blossom in early summer.

Yellow flowers are produced by the evergreen barberries but never in sufficient quantity to be showy. However, some of the dwarf species have other charms. The seldom offered *Berberis calliantha* is well worth seeking out. Not only does it bear some of the largest flowers in the genus, but the glossy deep green leaves have silvery-white backs. There is also a bonus of some crimson leaves in autumn. *Berberis candidula* is only a mite less good, being a little smaller in these respects and with less deep green foliage. *B.x. stenophylla* 'Corallina Compacta' is an exception, being grown for its coral buds and orange flowers.

Grey foliage with a silvery sheen is the hallmark of *Convolvulus cneorum*. The freely produced flowers are white but from pink flushed buds. A specimen in full bloom may not be brightly showy but it has quality and eye-catching appeal. It needs a sheltered sunny site, as do the sun roses (*Cistus*), a colourful genus perfect for dry, poor soils. Showiest of the dwarf members is *C.x. purpureus* with many maroon blotched rose-crimson, crinkled saucers each 6-7.5cm (2½-3in) in diameter. *C.x pulverulentus* 'Sunset' has somewhat smaller, non-blotched blooms of glowing magenta-pink and greyer leaves. *C.creticus* has even greyer foliage and smaller flowers that come near to being rose-pink, while the hybrids *C.x skanbergii* and 'Silver Pink' are a truer pink but of paler hue.

Lavender goes well with the sun roses and provides that rare hue among shrubs in general, blue. *Lavandula angustifolia* 'Vera', the so-called Dutch lavender, has the broadest, greyest leaves but rather pale flowers; 'Munstead' has the brightest and 'Hidcote' the deepest blue flowers. The French lavender, (*L.stoechas*) is usually dwarfer and each flower spike is topped by a dense tuft of ear-like deep purple bracts in summer.

For those with neutral to acid soil that does not dry out too rapidly there is a splendid array of colourful dwarf shrubs belonging to the heather family (*Ericaceae*). Heaths (*Erica*) and heathers (*Calluna*) have already been mentioned in the prostrate shrub section and many similar but taller varieties are readily available.

Of similar appeal but with larger leaves are *Andromeda* and *Daboecia*. *Andromeda polifolia* has leaves with rolled margins that are white beneath. In late spring and early summer they are topped by almost globular bells of sugar pink. Known as St Dabeoc's heath, *Daboecia cantabrica* also has leaves that are white beneath but the larger blooms are urn-shaped and rose-purple, white ('Alba') or bicoloured ('Bicolor'). It also has a longer season, odd spikes opening into autumn. *Kalmia angustifolia* 'Rubra' is a deep rose-red selection of the N.American sheep or dwarf laurel. It has bright green leaves and beautifully bowl-shaped blooms in clusters.

There are dozens of garden worthy dwarf rhododendrons; the following have colourful flowers, are easily grown and commercially available. All are evergreen. *R.fastigiatum* and *R.impeditum* in their best forms have blue-purple flowers over tiny neat leaves that are grey-green in the first mentioned. Small dark leaves and deep purple-blue flowers belong to *R.russatum* and what might be described as a yellow version is *R.chryseum*. *R.sanguineum* is bright crimson and *yakushimanum* has quite large white blooms that open from pink buds. It also has good foliage, silvery downy when young, buff downy beneath when mature.

Truer blue is found among the man-made hybrids: 'Augfast' (deep blue), 'Blue Bird' and 'Blue Tit' (pale blue). 'Chikor' has soft yellow flowers, usually with a touch of pink in bud while 'Princess Anne' is buttercup yellow; 'Ethel' has light crimson-scarlet blooms and those of 'Scarlet Wonder' are a deeper hue and prolifically borne; 'Pink Drift' is aptly named and very free with its flowers.

'Mikado' is something different, a salmon-orange evergreen azalea derived from the red-flowered Japanese *R.kaempferi*. Others in this group have red, pink, orange, mauve and purple-violet flowers.

Coloured foliage evergreens
Several shrubby veronicas (*Hebe*) have yellow or purple-flushed or variegated leaves and others come

ABOVE The richest-hued blue spiraea, *Caryopteris x clandonensis* 'Kew Blue'.
RIGHT *Cotoneaster horizontalis* combines an architectural habit with pleasing little pinkish flowers, followed by a profusion of red fruits.

in a variety of shades of green. A selection planted together make a satisfying feature if not colourful in the brightest sense. *H.odora* 'New Zealand Gold' has tiny box-like leaves that flush creamy yellow when young, though this varies somewhat depending on soil and site. *H*.x 'Waikiki' is flushed bronze-purple throughout the year and has blue-purple flowers as a bonus; *H.pimeleoides* 'Quicksilver' bears its tiny silvery-blue leaves on almost black stems – a striking contrast.

A group of *Hebe* species have tiny overlapping scale leaves and are known as whipcords. Becoming more popular is *H.ochracea* with cypress-like old gold foliage. It is often confused with *H.armstrongii*, but that species is yellow-green.

Woolly grey-white leaves are the attraction of *Ballota acetabulosa* while those of *B.pseudodictamnus* have a yellowish cast. Some nurseries and garden centres have these names mixed up. Common rue (*Ruta graveolens*) is worth growing for its blue-grey dissected leaves alone, but for that eye-catching touch *R.g.*'Variegata' has the foliage bordered and flushed deep cream.

Deciduous dwarfs The so-called blue spiraea (*Caryopteris* x *clandonensis*) is a deciduous member of that small, select band of shrubs with blue flowers. 'Ferndown' has deeper hued flowers and 'Kew Blue' is darker still. All have greyish-green aromatic leaves. Much nearer to true gentian blue is *Ceratostigma willmottianum*, a first rate shrub for a sheltered sunny spot. In autumn there is a bonus of some red leaves.

Showy yellow flowers are a feature of a group of St. John's worts often still listed as *Hypericum patulum*. Best known is the semi-evergreen 'Hidcote' and the hybrid *H.x moseranum*. Other names to look out for are *forrestii*, *henryi*, *kouytchense* and *prolificum*.

Most deutzias are too large for this category, but *D.compacta* 'Lavender Time' is a welcome dwarf with clusters of flowers that open lilac then turn lavender. Its close relative *Philadelphus* 'Manteau d'Hermine' has abundant creamy-white, double, fragrant blossoms. Other flowering genera worthy of consideration are *Fuchsia, Potentilla, Spiraea* and *Viburnum*. Rich red-purple foliage is provided by *Berberis thunbergii* 'Atropurpurea Nana' and the even smaller 'Bagatelle', while *B.t.*'Aurea' is a bright golden yellow.

Several small shrubs bear red berries but none better than the fishbone cotoneaster, *C.horizontalis*.

MEDIUM-SIZED SHRUBS

The medium-sized shrubs discussed below mainly come within the 1-2m (3 ¼-6½ft) range, though some will, in time exceed this. Shrubs of this height are of primary value. A few at least can be accommodated in the small garden and they are the most useful size for general planting where there is more room.

Flowering evergreens Many colourful and attractive shrubs come into this category and those that follow also have good foliage. A well grown specimen of the temperate South American zone, Darwin's barberry (*Berberis darwinii*) in full bloom is a sight to behold, its small, glossy, holly-like leaves being a perfect foil for the clusters of tiny bright orange-yellow flowers. A compatriot of *darwinii* and even more profuse in bloom, is *B.linearifolia* but it develops a rather gawky habit in time and is less effective on that score. The hybrid between them, *B.x lologensis* combines the parental characters most effectively.

Ghent azalea is a name given to a group of deciduous hybrid rhododendrons raised in Belgium and well-known for their prolifically-borne red, orange, pink or yellow flowers towards the end of May.

Most of the best *Ceanothus* species and cultivars come into the large shrub category, but two good ones that fit in here are 'Autumnal Blue' and 'Delight'. Both are among the hardiest of evergreen Californian lilacs, with dark green, smallish leaves and trusses of tiny, rich blue flowers; 'Delight' blooms in spring, 'Autumnal Blue' in late summer and autumn.

There are no reasonably hardy *Cistus* or sun roses with coloured flowers in this height category, but a freely blooming specimen of *C.ladanifer* is an eye-catching sight. Each pure white flower can reach 10cm (4in) across and a chocolate-crimson blotch highlights the base of each petal. The slightly hardier *C.x cyprius* is almost as good.

Big showy flowers are very much the hallmark of the camellias and they have handsome, glossy leaves of good size. *C.japonica* 'Apollo' has sumptuous semi-double scarlet flowers, while 'Elegans' is an elegant pink. 'Contessa Lavinia Maggi' is not quite sure what to do, producing double white, or pale pink blooms variously striped rose-cerise. 'Nagasaki' is another showy curiosity, with semi-double, white-marbled, rose-pink blooms and yellow mottled leaves.

Rhododendron is very much a companion of the camellias, both needing neutral to acid soil that does not dry out rapidly. Hundreds of different kinds come into this height category and only a few can be

LEFT *Elaeagnus pungens* 'Maculata' is one of the showiest of the yellow variegated evergreen shrubs. **BELOW** The young, red leaves of *Pieris formosa forrestii* 'Wakehurst'.

mentioned here. Patriotically named (though raised in Holland!) 'Britannia' is a thoroughly good, reliable garden plant with gloxinia-shaped crimson-scarlet flowers. 'Dairymaid' is creamy yellow with a red basal blotch, and 'Eldorado' has maroon-purple flowers lightened with a bright yellow blotch – a striking combination. 'Goldsworth Orange' is apricot-orange and 'Goldsworth Pink' a clear pink and free blooming. The rosy-purple 'Praecox' blooms in February and March, which makes it very desirable indeed.

Other evergreen flowering shrubs worthy of consideration are *Mahonia japonica, Daphne odora, Kalmia latifolia, Escallonia rubra* and *Ulex europaeus* 'Plenus' (double gorse).

Coloured-leaved evergreens Several species in this category have their young leaves in shades of red, equally showy, if not more so than some flowers. Outstanding is *Pieris formosa forrestii* 'Wakehurst', its young leaves rather like poinsettia bracts in their scarlet brilliance. It will exceed 2m (6½ft) in time but can be pruned. More compact and slower growing is *P.* 'Forest Flame' (or 'Flame of the Forest'). Several other good cultivars are listed, all with a bonus of sprays of small urn-shaped white flowers. Pieris belongs to the heather family and must have acid soil. *Photinia x fraseri* 'Red Robin' makes the same kind of impact in the garden scene and the leaves are larger. It is a member of the rose family and will grow in limy land.

Brightly variegated leaves are borne by several cultivars of *Euonymus japonicus*, common holly (*Ilex aquifolium*) and *Elaeagnus pungens*. Recommended are *Euonymus japonicus* 'Aureopictus', *Ilex aquifolium* 'Myrtifolia Aureomaculata' and *Elaeagnus pungens* 'Maculata', all very different but all with leaves carrying a central blotch of gold. Other cultivars have white, cream or yellow leaf margins.

Evergreen fruiters Most of the really good evergreen fruiters are large shrubs but the following are worth mentioning. *Skimmia japonica* has good foliage, fragrant off-white flowers and bright red berries, but male and female flowers are carried on separate plants so at least two are required. *Aucuba japonica*, usually known as spotted or Japanese laurel, is grown as a foliage plant though the spotted leaves are not to everybody's liking. If male and female plants are grown together a crop of large, lustrous red berries can be expected. For the best results, the glossy plain green leaved aucubas should be chosen, notably 'Crassifolia' (male) and 'Longifolia' (female). If the yellow-spotted cultivars are preferred, then go for 'Crotonifolia' (male) and 'Gold Dust' (female). Both are thickly gold spotted.

The many varieties of *Cotoneaster* are renowned as berry-bearing shrubs of easy culture. *C.salicifolia floccosus* has willow-like, veiny leaves and prolific clusters of red berries. It can exceed 2m (6½ft) in time. *C.franchetii* and its variety *sternianus* are semi-evergreen with oval leaves sage green above, white-downy beneath; the fruits are orange-red.

Deciduous flowering shrubs The 1-2m (1¼-6½ft) height range includes some of the best known and colourful shrubs; for example, buddleia, species roses, kerria, weigela, hydrangea, forsythia and japonica. For those with an acid soil, the hybrid deciduous azaleas are a must. There are several cultivar groups derived from crossing together *Rhododendron luteum, japonicum, calendulaceum, occidentale* and others. Very reliable is the Knap Hill Group, particularly the following: 'Balzac' (orange-red), 'Berry-rose' (pink with yellow blotch), 'Harvest Moon' (pale yellow), 'Homebush' (double, deep carmine) and 'Satan' (deep scarlet).

Rosa hugonis bears lightly fragrant pale yellow flowers in May, to be followed by the richer toned 'Canary Bird'. *R.virginiana* is a suckering species to about 1.2m (4ft) with lustrous leaves that turn crimson in autumn and cerise-pink blooms in summer. Also suckering and with handsome foliage is the ramanas rose (*R.rugosa*). It has fragrant flowers to 10cm (4in) wide from summer to autumn. All cultivars are good, from the purple-red wild type to the pale rose-pink 'Frau Dagmar Hastrup', and double crimson-purple 'Roseraie de l'Hay'. All have large, tomato-red hips.

Hardy hibiscus can be superb in late summer and early autumn, especially if the season has been warm. *H.syriacus* 'Blue Bird' is violet-blue with a darker eye and the best of its colour; 'Duc de Brabant' has double blooms of deep rose-purple, while 'Woodbridge' is deep rose-pink with a darker centre. Though hardy they all like a warm site and then bloom prolifically.

Hydrangea to most people means the mop-headed so-called Hortensias. They are certainly colourful and well worth growing but the more elegant Lace-cap group of cultivars should also be tried. Especially fine are 'Blue Wave' (pink on limy soils, blue on acid ones) and *H.serrata* 'Rosalba' (white to crimson). For very large handsome leaves and blue and white lacecap heads, try *H.sargentiana*, a splendid shade specimen, that grows in sun also.

Common lilac comes into the large shrubs category but there are smaller species and hybrids, notably *Syringa microphylla* 'Superba'. This

RIGHT The hardy *Hibiscus syriacus* 'Blue Bird' makes an eye-catching specimen shrub with its flowers of deep violet-blue.
FAR RIGHT *Philadelphus coronarius*.'Aureus' combines fragrant white flowers with sunny yellow foliage.

has small oval leaves and trusses of rose-pink flowers not only in May but intermittently until autumn.

Deutzias now come in a variety of pink, purple and white shades, are easy to grow and reliable in bloom. *D*.'Contraste' and 'Magicien' have starry mauve-pink flowers darker in bud; X *kalmiiflora* is white flushed carmine and 'Mont Rose' opens large blooms of rose-pink.

One magnolia just gets into our height range. This is *M.stellata*, the Japanese star magnolia, fairly easy growing and free blooming from an early age. It is white but still very showy; 'Rosea' is soft pink.

Some tree paeonies produce the largest flowers of all hardy shrubs, but they need shelter from late spring frosts and screening from the hottest summer sun. When happily situated they are real show stoppers. Easiest of all is the species *Paeonia lutea ludlowii* with flowers up to 10cm (4in) or more across. Hybrids between *lutea* and the larger Chinese *suffruticosa* have given us several huge bloomed cultivars, some of them double. Good examples are 'Aurora' semi-double, coppery-red; 'Alice Harding' double, canary yellow and 'Souvenir de Maxime Cornu', extra large double, yellow edged and shaded salmon-carmine. *P.suffruticosa* itself has produced many cultivars in shades of pink, red, purple and white.

Deciduous shrubs with coloured-leaves The so-called smoke tree or bush (*Cotinus coggygria*) has bright green leaves and smoky fawn-pink flower clusters; pleasing but not colourful. On the other hand *C.c.* 'Rubrifolius' has red leaves, almost translucent in bright light. 'Royal Purple' and 'Notcutt's' have deep purple leaves that contrast most strikingly with the yellow foliage of *Philadelphus coronarius* 'Aureus', *Ribes sanguineum* 'Brocklebankii', or the plumed golden elderberry (*Sambucus racemosa* 'Plumosa Aurea').

Bright summer variegated leaves are provided by some of the dogwoods, in particular *Cornus alba* 'Elegantissima' (white variegated) and 'Spaethii' (yellow).

Berried shrubs Several shrubs are renowned for their profuse crops of colourful fruits, notably *Cotoneaster bullatus, divaricatus* and *wardii;* *Berberis x carminea* 'Buccaneer', x *rubrostilla* and *thunbergii; Euonymus europaeus* 'Red Cascade'; *Callicarpa giraldii, Viburnum opulus* and *betulifolium* and various roses.

LARGE SHRUBS

For the purposes of this book, large shrubs are those 2-3m (6½-10ft) or more in height. They are too big for tiny gardens and the least useful for average sized plots, although one to a few can be used most effectively as specimens. Only in gardens of ¼ acre and above should they be planted with any freedom.

Ceanothus x 'Puget Blue' received the Award of Merit from the Royal Horticultural Society in 1971.

Flowering evergreens In all but the most sheltered sites, *Abutilon vitifolium* is semi-evergreen, but even if rather thinly disposed on the branches, the large, greyish, maple-like leaves are handsome. However, the glory of this large Chilean shrub is its profusion of 6-8cm (2½-3¼in) wide saucer-shaped flowers of satiny mauve. 'Veronica Tennant' has more richly tinted flowers and needs a sheltered site. Of more slender growth, with smaller leaves and darker flowers is the hybrid *A.x suntense*.

Also from temperate S.America and semi-evergreen is *Buddleia globosa*, often very prosaically called the orange ball tree. It has dark green, finely wrinkled leaves which are a handsome background for the tiny orange flowers arranged in tight balls. It makes a fine contrast planted with a late spring-blooming ceanothus, a genus renowned for its blue flowers. One of the best of these is *C.impressus* with tiny dark green leaves having deeply impressed veins. The deep blue flowers are carried in abundance. Slightly darker in colour but with bigger leaves is its hybrid cultivar 'Puget Blue'. Often topping 3m (10ft) is *C.thyrsiflorus* a very free blooming species with lustrous oval leaves.

Although white flowers cannot be described as colourful, when they are of large size or carried in quantity they can catch the eye as no colour can. *Magnolia grandiflora*, the N.American bull-bay can achieve tree size but it takes a long time to do so and for many years behaves as a large shrub. Its highly glossed oval leaves range from 15-25cm (6-10in) in length and are very handsome. The great waterlily-like flowers have a similar size range; largest of all in the cultivar 'Goliath'. *Eucryphia x nymansensis*, eventually makes a small, dense columnar tree, but behaves as a bush for 10-15 years. In late summer the dark evergreen foliage can be almost covered with sizeable four-petalled white flowers.

Pale grey can never be described as colourful either, but the silk tassel bush (*Garrya elliptica*) when covered with its 15-25cm (6-10in) long catkins can be a striking sight indeed. Only the male plant is worth growing for this purpose and the selected form 'James Roof' has the longest catkins, to 35cm (14in).

Colour is certainly provided by the *Camellia* and *Rhododendron* genera. Many *C.japonica* cultivars exceed 3m (10ft) but take some years to do so. Very garden worthy is the hybrid group known as *C.x williamsii*, having generally slightly smaller flowers than *japonica* but in greater abundance. Recommended are 'Donation' and 'November Pink', the latter valuable in starting to flower in late autumn if the weather is mild. *Rhododendron thomsonii* has large waxy-crimson bells and *R.x* Hawk 'Crest' has yellow ones, while the *R.cinnabarinum* hybrid 'Royal Flush' bears its plum-crimson, yellow flushed blooms often in the greatest prodigality. There are many more available from nurseries and garden centres.

Coloured evergreen foliage and fruit In a hard winter, *Cotoneaster* x 'Cornubia' is only semi-evergreen. When heavily fruited however, the leaves are hidden by glossy red berries. It is perhaps the best and most reliable of large fruiting shrubs and the leaves and flowers are pleasing also. All the tall-growing firethorns are equally free-fruiting but their habit is less graceful. Recommended are *Pyracantha atalantioides* and *P.rogersiana*, the latter having a bright yellow-berried form 'Flava'.

Arbutus unedo 'Rubra', the pink flowered strawberry tree, is a must, having good foliage, pretty little urn-shaped pink flowers and round, red fruits (not really like strawberries), all together in autumn.

ABOVE The waxy crimson flowers and glossy evergreen leaves of *Rhododendron thomsonii*.
LEFT Considering its California homeland *Garrya elliptica* is astonishingly hardy.

Flowering deciduous shrubs Several of the best winter flowering shrubs come into this category. All can be pruned to keep them near to the 2m (6½ft) mark but are best if allowed to achieve their natural sizes and shapes. *Viburnum farreri* (*fragrans*) is erect in habit at least when young, with pleasing, prominently veined leaves. From late autumn until the following spring, depending on prevailing temperatures, the twig tips bear clusters of fragrant white flowers from pink-tinted buds. The hybrid *V.x bodnantense* is larger in all its parts and faster growing. If possible, the cultivar 'Deben' with pinker buds should be obtained.

The witch hazels (*Hamamelis*) provide yellow (though some of the newer sorts are red or coppery-orange). Best of all is *H.mollis* 'Pallida', its large starry flowers a bright sulphur yellow and most welcome during the late December to March period. All the *mollis* forms are good, with a bonus of yellow autumn leaves.

Unless one can obtain the 'Luteus' cultivar of *Chimonanthus praecox* (*fragrans*), this shrub, known also as wintersweet, cannot rank as colourful. However, being powerfully fragrant and blooming in winter, it is a must for a sheltered wall, where there is room.

For late spring and early summer, several of the finest shrubs in this category are at their best. *Cornus florida* is one, producing tight clusters of tiny flowers surrounded by four large petal-like bracts. These may be white ('White Cloud'), pink

ABOVE *Malus sieboldii* is one of the very few shrubby, flowering crab apples. RIGHT *Viburnum farreri* flowers in winter.

('Apple Blossom'), or rose-red ('Cherokee Chief'). The foliage colours richly in autumn.

The crab apples (*Malus*) are mostly small to medium sized trees but a few stay as large bushes. The most beautiful and the largest of these is *M.floribunda* with dense clouds of crimson-budded, blush blossom followed by little red and yellow crab apples. More shrubby are the similar *M.sargentii* and *sieboldii*. The latter has pink budded flowers, the former is all white. Both have red, cherry-like crabs, but those of *sieboldii* may also be yellow.

Forsythia (spring bell) and *Syringa* (lilac) are too well known to need mentioning in detail, but both shrubs have less well known cultivars worth trying. Look out for *Forsythia suspensa atrocaulis*, its almost black stems contrasting well with the pale yellow flowers. *Syringa vulgaris* 'Primrose' is a delightful true yellow lilac, while 'Sensation' really is – the red-purple petals having a white edge.

Among the tall shrub roses, *Rosa moyesii* takes some beating. Not only does it have sizeable glowing crimson flowers, but large, flagon-shaped red hips to carry colour into autumn.

Colourful foliage and fruits Some of the brightest foliage occurs as it slowly dies, in autumn, the breakdown of the chlorophyll revealing red and yellow pigments in various combinations. Although snowy mespilus (*Amelanchier*) is grown equally for its profusion of white flowers and red-yellow-orange autumn tints, the latter makes the greatest impact. The commonest species is *A.lamarckii*, often sold as *A.canadensis*. Both colour well, as does *A.laevis* which has delicate pink young foliage.

The American *Cotinus obovata* provides spectacular autumn tints, with a bonus of bronze-pink foliage in spring.

Another brilliant autumn performer is *Cotinus obovatus* (*americanus*), its leaves taking on shades of orange, scarlet and purple; and there is a bonus of unfurling bronze-pink foliage in spring. Moist acid soil gives the best results. Many other shrubs have autumn colour, including *Rhus typhina* and *R.t.* 'Laciniata', *Hamamelis*, *Corylopsis*, *Euonymus*, *Crataegus*, *Rhododendron* (deciduous azaleas) and *Aesculus parviflora*.

Crab apples and rose hips and other colourful fruits mentioned above are part of the delights of the autumn and winter scene and at least a few should be in every garden. Among those to consider are sea buckthorn (*Hippophae rhamnoides*). Provided that at least one male and one to several female bushes are planted a wealth of orange berries can be expected. The silvery shaded foliage is also attractive. Not easy to obtain but well worth looking for is the sapphire berry, *Symplocos paniculata* (*crataegoides*), a tall shrub with bright blue berries.

CULTIVATION

On the whole, shrubs are particularly easy going plants. Rich soil is not necessary; indeed, it is likely to stimulate strong vigorous growth at the expense of flowers or colourful autumn foliage. Ordinary, or even poor soils give good results with a minimum of preparation, providing there is adequate moisture. However, some shrubs do have particular preferences. For example, most members of the heather family (*Ericaceae*) need an acid soil, and several other shrub genera prefer a rooting medium with very little lime. An acid soil is one with very little free lime. Simple, cheap kits for testing the acidity/alkalinity of soils are obtainable at garden centres.

Preparation Unless one takes over a garden that has been well maintained, some preparation of the soil will be necessary before planting. A first consideration is to eradicate perennial weeds, specially the strangling bindweeds which can be such a nuisance among trees and shrubs. Use one of the modern herbicides to clean up the site well beforehand. If the plot is rough grass, beds and borders can be marked out with a total weedkiller such as 'Weedol'.

Amelanchier lamarckii parades in gardens as *A. canadensis* and colours reliably every autumn. This medium to large sized shrub appreciates a moist site.

Apart from the planting holes – or trench for a hedge – it is not usually necessary to dig over the whole site, but there are exceptions. You may be unlucky enough to take over a new garden which has been stripped of its top soil, or contains lots of builders' rubbish, in which case, the site must be roughly forked over, the rubbish removed and more top soil brought in. Subsoil can be made into a fertile growing medium but it needs lots of bulky, humus-forming material, such as 'Forest Bark' Ground and Composted, rotted manure, mushroom compost, garden compost, peat or leafmould, worked into it and spread on the surface. A load of topsoil is usually cheaper.

If the garden area is poorly drained it is seldom worth going to the expense of installing a drainage system and soakaways. Remember, if there is not a nearby ditch, a soakaway is seldom adequate to take all the drainage water in winter. The alternative is to choose shrubs that tolerate wet conditions.

Planting Autumn to spring is the best time for planting, though containerised specimens can be planted out whenever the soil and weather are suitable. In winter, mild weather when the soil is not too wet is best. In areas where spring droughts occur fairly regularly, evergreens are best planted in autumn, the earlier the better. Dig each hole slightly larger than the root ball of the plant, add a couple of handfuls of fertilizer such as bonemeal, and set the containerised plant so that when the hole is filled in, the top of the ball is covered with about 2.5cm (1in) of soil. Plants direct from the nursery ground should be placed slightly deeper than they were, with the roots spread out as evenly as possible. Fill in the hole and firm with fists or feet (depending on the size of the plant). Leave a shallow depression around the plant for watering, especially on free-draining soils.

Maintenance Weeding and watering are the most important maintenance activities for the next two years or so while the shrubs get thoroughly established. Unless the soil is of a water retentive nature, such as a clay type, start watering in late spring after two or three weeks without rain. Fill up the depressions three times then leave them for a week and repeat, and so on.

During this establishment period, an annual spring mulch of 'Forest Bark' Ground and Composted is very beneficial. Not only will it keep the soil moist and cool but it virtually eliminates weeds. On poor soil, a mulch of this kind should be applied at least every other year, ideally with a light dressing of a fertilizer such as Growmore added at the same time.

Shrubs do not need staking unless an already well grown specimen is transplanted. In a windy site a short stake is advisable to prevent wind rocking, until established. Remove the stake as soon as the shrub is firmly rooted again, usually in one to two years.

Pruning Although this may seem heresy, all shrubs will grow and flower without being pruned. However, some species keep a more shapely habit and/or bloom more reliably if pruned annually, or at least from time to time.

Certain shrubs, notably philadelphus, deutzia, weigela and others of similar vigorous habit, get congested after several years and certainly benefit if a few of the oldest stems at the base are removed annually in winter.

To maintain a more compact shape and floriferous state, stems that have flowered can be cut back by half to three quarters, or even down to the lowest node on big shrubs. For late winter to early summer flowering species, the best time to do this is immediately the last bloom withers or falls. For the mid summer to autumn flowerers, pruning must take place from late autumn to early spring.

Dig a hole rather wider and deeper than the rootball of containerised shrub. Add peat and a little bonemeal.

Carefully remove container; set shrub in the hole so that the top of rootball is about 4cm (1½in) below soil surface.

Fill in around the plant with soil and firm well in but leave a shallow depression to facilitate watering.

PROPAGATION

There is a lot of satisfaction to be gained from propagating one's own shrubs. Some of the most colourful sorts root with ease from cuttings and grow fast, blooming within a year. Even among those slower or more difficult to propagate there are many which grow strongly once they have established a good root system.

Although cuttings provide the easiest means of propagating most shrubs, layering is a surer means for a few. All shrubs which produce seeds can also be raised by this means, but many, if not all the cultivated varieties are unlikely to come true to type. Some species vary also and it is necessary to raise a batch of plants and pick one or two of the best. Nevertheless, raising them from seed is undoubtedly the most rewarding method of propagating shrubs for the garden, provided that you have the necessary patience.

Cuttings There are several different sorts of cuttings but here we are concerned with those made from stems of one growing season or less. There are three categories based on maturity:
- Softwood refers to sappy, recently formed stems with actively growing tips.
- Semi-hardwood are those which are becoming woody at the base.
- Hardwood are fully woody stems at the end of the growing season.
The last two categories are the most useful to the shrub enthusiast.

Many good garden shrubs are easily raised from hardwood cuttings:
1. Remove newly matured stems in autumn at, or soon after, leaf fall.
2. Cut the stems into 20-25cm (8-10in) lengths, but do not use the soft tips.
3. Dig out a narrow trench, about 12.5-15cm (5-6in) deep, in a well-drained soil and in a sheltered site. If the soil is on the heavy side, place a 2cm (¾in) layer of sharp sand in the bottom. Set the cuttings vertically in the trench, spacing them 20-30cm (8-12in) apart.
4. Fill in with soil and carefully firm with your foot. Add a little more soil to make level.

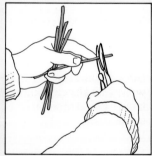

There are two methods of preparing cuttings: with and without heels. Nodal cuttings are lengths of stem cut cleanly below a leaf or node. Heel cuttings are lateral or side stems carefully pulled or cut from the parent stem so that they have a wedge or sliver of older tissue at the base. Quite often a 'tail' of the older stem comes away and this must be trimmed off, along with any leaves that may happen to be growing near to it.

All cuttings must be reduced to an optimum length which, though varying from species to species, ranges from 6-13cm (2½-5in) for semi-hardwood, and 20-30cm (8-12in) for hardwood. Semi-hardwood cuttings are reduced by removing the soft tips. They are taken in late summer or early autumn, dipped in 'Keriroot' hormone rooting powder and placed in cuttings compost in a propagating frame. Bottom heat is

The glossy, red young stems of *Cornus alba* 'Sibirica' glow in the sunset light of a late autumn day. This spectacular looking shrub will succeed in wet or dry soil and forms a positive thicket of stems to provide welcome colour late in the year. It will benefit greatly from hard pruning in the early spring of every alternate year. Other than that it will make few demands in terms of cultivation.

an advantage but not essential for success. A rooting powder such as 'Keriroot' with added fungicide is beneficial, usually resulting in a higher percentage of rooted cuttings that will make healthy growth.

Hardwood cuttings are taken in autumn and early winter and inserted in well drained, ideally sandy soil, outside. A sheltered site is best and watering is necessary during dry spells in spring and early summer. One last piece of advice – don't forget to label the cuttings.

A spray of newly matured holly shoots in early autumn; ideal cuttings material.

Layering All shrubs can be layered and if only one to a few young plants are required, this is the method to use. Late summer and spring are the best times. A low branch is chosen or, if necessary, one is pulled down and tied or pinned into position. One year old stems from this branch are bent into a U-shape so that the bottom of the U can be buried shallowly. The soil is loosened, a hole made and sand worked into the bottom of the hole. Then the stem is nicked, dusted with rooting powder and buried about 5cm (2in) deep. A forked stick or bent wire will hold it in place or it can be secured to a cane. One year later, the layer can be severed and transplanted.

Seeds With the exception of the heather family, most shrub seeds are easily dealt with. A standard seed compost is suitable and no artificial heat required. The seeds should be sown when ripe, or as soon as received, and placed in a cold frame so you can control the amount of rainfall they receive. As only a few plants will be needed, 6-10cm (2½-4in) pots or pans are ideal. The seed is sown thinly, pressed into the surface and covered with 1cm (⅖in) of fine grit. Seeds in berries should be squeezed out and sown directly.

Seedlings should be pricked off as soon as they are large enough to handle. They can be grown on in pots but usually grow bigger if planted out in a nursery plot.

Seeds of the heather family, such as *Pieris, Kalmia, Rhododendron,* are dust-like and must be sown in spring on an acid substrate. Best results are obtained if pure, moist sphagnum peat or finely chopped living sphagnum moss is used. Sow the seed thinly on the surface and do not cover. Place in a propagating case or in a plastic bag or box. Bottom heat is beneficial. Prick off seedlings the following spring.

32

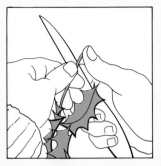

Having selected a healthy lateral stem and carefully removed it from the parent stem, trim the 'tail' of tissue from 'heel'.

Remove the lower leaves on either side of the cutting and dip the cut end in a rooting powder to facilitate rooting.

Having prepared a bed of sandy soil in a cold frame, make a hole with a dibber and insert the cutting.

A spray of the shrub *Ceanothus impressus*, bearing a number of suitable shoots ideal for use as cuttings.

As with the holly cutting shown above, remove a few lower leaves and dip each cutting in rooting powder.

With a dibber, make holes at regular intervals round a pot of sandy compost, then insert and firm in the cuttings.

Using a pair of tweezers is the most efficient and least messy way to remove seeds from a fleshy fruit.

Directly they are removed from the berry, sow the seeds as shown, in a proprietary seed-sowing compost.

Once sown, most shrub seeds are best covered with grit, then placed in a cold frame, or outside.

PESTS AND DISEASES

Shrubs are fairly free from pests and diseases but from time to time they fall prey to some of the commoner plant pathogens, i.e. aphids (greenfly), capsid bug, caterpillars, mildew and honey fungus. When using the insecticides and fungicides recommended here, make sure to follow exactly the makers' instructions. An overdose may scorch or damage the plant as well as killing the pests; an underdose is likely to have no effect at all.

Here are the problems to keep a lookout for, and the action to take if they occur. Wherever spraying is recommended as a treatment, always take care not to spray open flowers or buds as you work.

Leaves and shoot tips deformed
This condition is usually the result of aphids (green- and blackfly), tiny, soft, oval creatures with or without wings and invariably in colonies.

'Sybol' and 'Rapid' are effective insecticides. If young leaves also look somewhat tattered or have irregular holes, then capsid bugs are present. These are like larger, fast moving aphids and the damage is done to immature shoot tips long

Pests and diseases appear in the most well-ordered gardens, but they can be kept in check. Damaged leaves, as on this *Clerodendrum* can indicate problems.

before it is noticed. Where damage is frequent and regular, spray at two weekly intervals during the growing season with 'Sybol'.

Leaves eaten Pieces eaten out of leaves indicate that a caterpillar, beetle or earwig has been feeding. Earwigs, and the vine- and clay-coloured weevils feed at night and can be controlled by spraying with 'Sybol'. Alternatively, earwigs can be trapped in rolls of corrugated cardboard, or small containers of straw, or dry, dead leaves. These must be checked daily and the insects destroyed. Large-scale caterpillar damage is best controlled by spraying with 'Picket' or 'Sybol'. If the feeding is irregular and slime trails are present, slugs or snails are the culprits. Apply ICI Slug Pellets containing metaldehyde.

Leaves mottled A lightish, fine mottling, often with total yellowing and premature fall is likely to be red spider mite, if the shrubs are growing near warm, sheltered walls. Spray red spider with 'Sybol'. If the mottling is on rhododendrons and there are also rusty brown marks on the leaf undersides this is caused by rhododendron bug; use 'Sybol' at fortnightly intervals from mid-June to August.

Leaves withered Some *Pyracantha* and *Cotoneaster* leaf and flower clusters may wither, turn brown and hang. This may be the bacterial disease fireblight, mainly a trouble of apples and pears. Its presence must be reported to a local officer of the Ministry of Agriculture, Fisheries and Food. All infected branches must be burnt. If entire branches or plants suffer this collapse or withering of foliage, see the entry Whole plant dying.

Leaves with 'sooty' film Occasionally a blackish film appears on the leaves of shrubs growing beneath trees, lime (*Tilia*) in particular. The tree is suffering a plague of aphids which, as they feed, secrete a sugary liquid known as honey dew. This rains down on the shrub leaves and is then colonised by a minute fungus known as sooty mould. The only cure is to kill the aphids or transplant the shrubs.

Stems and leaf backs with brown scales Shrubs grown against sheltered walls may suffer tiny, oval, glossy humpback or even smaller flattened, narrow scale insects, often in colonies. These suck sap and weaken the plant if they are abundant. Control by spraying with 'Sybol', two or three times at two weekly intervals from late spring. Fully deciduous shrubs can also be sprayed in winter, with a tar acid emulsion such as 'Clean-Up'.

Whole or part of plant suddenly dying Occasionally, a well grown shrub or a large part of it dies comparatively suddenly, the leaves withering and browning. If left, clusters of honey-coloured toadstools appear at the base of the plant, giving the disease its name of honey fungus. When the plant is dug up, there is usually a sheet of whitish fungal tissue at the base of the stem just below ground level and among the dead or dying roots there are blackish strands that suggest its alternative name of bootlace fungus. There is no absolute cure for this but drenching the infected areas with Bray's Emulsion can kill existing disease and protect healthy plants from infection if they are sprayed annually. Do not replant into treated soil for at least eight months.

SIXTY OF THE BEST

The following have been selected to provide a colourful shrub garden or to act as a background for smaller plants. One item from each of the 12 lists will give year-round interest in a small garden; all 60 will create a shrub garden to be proud of. All are commercially available, though a few will need to be searched for.

COLOURFUL SPRING FOLIAGE

Aesculus neglecta
'Erythroblastos'. Although
eventually a large deciduous shrub
or even a small bushy tree, this
horse-chestnut is slow growing and
will take 20-30 years to get big. The
hand-shaped leaves unfurl a lovely,
deep salmon-pink which ages to pale
yellow-green.

Pieris x
'Forest Flame' ('Flame of the
Forest'). This hybrid between the
evergreen *P.formosa forrestii*
'Wakehurst' and *P.japonica* is
hardier than its *formosa* parent but
has equally brilliant red young
foliage and the white urn-shaped
flowers, in drooping panicles, are a
pleasing bonus. It forms a large
shrub in time.

Photinia x fraseri.
This member of the rose family is a
large evergreen shrub, not unlike a
larger-leaved *Pieris* and also has red
young leaves, but it thrives on
alkaline soil, whereas *Pieris* must
have an acid rooting medium to
thrive. *P.x f.* 'Robusta' has coppery-
red leaves, 'Red Robin' bright red.

Sambucus racemosa
'Plumosa Aurea'. The elegantly
dissected leaves of this deciduous
shrub are rich yellow when young,
fading to a paler yellow as they
mature. The flower clusters also are
yellow.

Spiraea japonica (bumalda)
'Goldflame'. This small deciduous
shrub has its youngest leaves
coppery-red, then turning to yellow
and finally maturing yellow-green.
Flattened clusters of crimson
flowers open in summer.

Pieris 'Flame of the Forest'

38

Aesculus neglecta
'Erythroblastos'

Sambucus racemosus
'Plumosa Aurea'

Spiraea japonica 'Goldflame'

COLOURFUL SUMMER AND ALL YEAR FOLIAGE

Aralia elata
'Variegata'. One of the finest, large, deciduous specimen shrubs, this aralia has sparsely branching, very robust stems set with a scattering of small prickles. The handsome compound leaves can exceed 90cm (3ft) in length and are composed of creamy-white margined, oval leaflets. Branched clusters of globular, white flower heads open in autumn.

Cotinus coggygria
'Foliis Purpureis'. Known as the purple-leaved smoke bush, this large deciduous shrub has rich red-purple leaves, brightest when young. 'Notcutt's' selection is even darker. The smoky flowering and seeding heads are reddish-pink.

Ilex x altaclarensis
'Lawsoniana'. Larger leaved and more vigorous than common holly, this big evergreen cultivar has leaves with bright golden yellow centres. If a male holly is nearby, it will also produce red berries.

Pittosporum tenuifolium
'Silver Queen'. Ultimately a large evergreen shrub, but easily kept smaller by pruning or clipping, it has leaves suffused and bordered with creamy white. It needs a sheltered situation which does not suffer prolonged hard frost; makes a good tub specimen if brought under cover in winter.

Weigela florida
'Variegata'. This small deciduous shrub has dual purpose attractions, cream-bordered, bright green leaves and pink, foxglove-shaped flowers in early summer.

Aralia elata 'Variegata'

Cotinus coggygria 'Foliis Purpureis'

Ilex x altaclarensis 'Lawsoniana'

AUTUMN FOLIAGE

Euonymus alatus
'Compactus'. When not in leaf this small to medium-sized deciduous shrub displays slender stems with broad corky wings. The leaves turn rich red, accompanied by pink fruits. Best in acid to neutral soils.

Fothergilla major.
This medium-sized deciduous shrub is one of the most brilliant autumn colouring performers, yellow to rich red. In spring, just as the leaf buds break into growth it also bears a display of white, bottle-brush shaped flower clusters.

Hamamelis japonica.
Very much a dual-purpose plant, this large deciduous shrub has spidery yellow flowers on bare branches in winter and rich yellow autumn leaves.

Rhus typhina.
Also know as stag's horn sumach, this popular shrub has ash-like leaves that turn shades of yellow, orange and red. The brown furry stems bear red flower clusters.

Rosa virginiana (lucida).
Although rarely above 1.2-1.5m (4-5ft) and sometimes less, this handsome rose suckers widely to form dome-shaped thickets. The glossy, deciduous leaves make a good background for the crimson-pink blooms, and in autumn turn bright shades of orange and crimson.

Rosa virginiana

Hamamelis japonica

onymus alatus 'Compactus'

SPRING FLOWERING

Camellia x
'Inspiration'. This hybrid between the common *C.japonica* and the rarely grown, more tender *C.reticulata*, is a medium-sized evergreen of great charm, producing large, semi-double, deep pink flowers against rich green foliage.

Corylopsis platypetala.
Medium to large in size, this deciduous species bears pendent spikes of pale yellow, fragrant flowers before the foliage. The deep green oval leaves are tinted blue-white beneath and usually colour in autumn.

Magnolia x soulangiana.
Best known of all magnolias and easiest to please, this hybrid was raised in France early in the 19th century by the nurseryman Mons. Soulange-Bodin. There are several cultivars, ranging from 'Alba Superba' (pure white) to 'Rustica Rubra' (rich rosy red).

Syringa vulgaris 'Souvenir de Louis Spaeth'

Syringa vulgaris.
The common lilac is one of the showiest of all large deciduous shrubs for a late spring display. There are many cultivars, double and single-flowered, in shades of white, cream, yellow, lilac, purple and almost blue. All are fragrant.

Viburnum carlesii
'Aurora'. This is the most colourful cultivar of a medium-sized deciduous shrub renowned for its richly scented flowers. As a bonus, the autumn leaves often take on red and yellow tints.

SUMMER FLOWERING

Aesculus parviflora.
Although a 'miniature' horse-chestnut, this suckering species is a large shrub often wider than tall. In late summer and early autumn it produces airy bottle brushes of white flowers with pink-tipped stamens. In autumn the leaves turn yellow.

Hydrangea macrophylla
Hortensia. Under this name are grouped the many familiar hydrangeas with magnificent mop heads of blue, purple, red, pink and white. Kept regularly pruned they can be classed as small deciduous shrubs, but left to grow naturally they eventually come into the medium category. For a change, try the Lacecap cultivars with their more elegant 'lacy' flower heads. True blue colouring only develops on acid soil. On limy land use one of the proprietary blueing compounds.

Hydrangea 'Blue Wave'

42

Kolkwitzia amabilis.
Although large and sometimes untidy, this deciduous shrub is one of the most glorious in bloom, producing a profusion of pink, yellow-throated flowers. 'Pink Cloud' is the best cultivar. Its vernacular name of beauty bush is well deserved.

Lavatera olbia

Lavatera olbia
'Rosea'. This colourful bush mallow is semi-evergreen and medium-sized. From summer to late autumn it produces a succession of large, widely funnel-shaped, bright lilac-pink flowers. Hard annual pruning each spring gives the best results.

Potentilla fruticosa.
Tolerant and easy going, this variable shrub is one of the most useful and attractive in the small deciduous group. Of rounded habit, it has tiny, fingered leaves and flowers like small single roses in shades of yellow, orange, red, cream, pink and white.

COLOURFUL FRUITS

Clerodendrum trichotomum fargesii.
Medium to large and deciduous, this is a shrub of quality that deserves to be seen more often. It thrives well in limy soils. In late summer and autumn, white fragrant flowers in starry maroon-red calyces open in profusion. When the flowers fall, the red calyces remain to highlight bright blue berries.

Cotoneaster x
'Cornubia'. This familiar, semi-evergreen large shrub is one of the best for an abundant red berry display, and summer borne creamy-white flowers.

Euonymus latifolius.
Medium to sometimes large in size, this spindle bush combines attractive red fruits with colourful autumn foliage.

Euonymus latifolius

Pyracantha rogersiana.
Although there are several excellent firethorns, some of them comparatively recent hybrids, this wild species collected in 1911, in China, is still one of the best. Large and evergreen, it has a profusion of white flowers in summer and scarlet berries in autumn and winter (birds permitting). *P.r.*'Flava' has yellow fruits.

Viburnum rhytidophyllum.
Handsome and worth growing for its lustrous deep green leaves alone, this large evergreen also has creamy white flowers and red berries that finally turn black. The hybrid *V.x rhytidophylloides* is more vigorous and has broader leaves.

COLOURFUL STEMS

Cornus alba sibirica.
The winter twigs of this deciduous, medium-sized shrub are glistening red. To maintain a thicket of young stems, fairly hard annual or biennial pruning must be carried out. The oval leaves, cream flowers and white berries are pleasing but not outstanding.

Cornus stolonifera
'Flaviramea'. Very similar in its summer appearance to *Cornus alba* and also medium sized and suckering, this shrub has very effective, bright, greenish-yellow winter twigs.

Leycesteria formosa.
Rather unhelpfully known as Himalayan honeysuckle, this erect, hollow stemmed shrub is usually grown for its pendent spikes of reddish bracts and white tubular flowers. However, pruned hard each spring (this also produces the largest flower spikes) it provides a sheaf of robust, 2m (6½ft) tall, bright green stems all winter.

Rubus biflorus.
This Himalayan deciduous, medium-sized 'raspberry' is a suckering shrub with prickly stems that in winter especially, appear as if whitewashed. It is a noteworthy plant for a shady site.

Salix alba
'Chermesina' ('Britzensis'). Allowed to grow naturally, this form of the white willow becomes a tree. To enjoy the one year old bright orange-red twigs however, it must be stooled (cut back to ground level) or pollarded annually in spring. It then behaves as a medium to large deciduous shrub.

SHRUBS FOR SHADY SITES

Aucuba japonica
'Crotonifolia'. The spotted-leaved Japanese laurels of the Victorian shrub borders are now returning to popularity and certainly brighten up shady places. 'Crotonifolia' is a male plant. If grown alongside the similar leaved but female 'Gold Dust' or 'Variegata Maculata' a bonus of large red fruits can be expected.

Hypericum calycinum.
The rose of Sharon is a favourite ground-cover plant but it is very invasive and must be used with care. A dwarf evergreen, with large yellow flowers, it looks fine beneath trees.

Rubus biflorus

Mahonia x
'Undulata'. Much like a taller Oregon grape, *M.aquifolium*, this medium-sized shrub has highly lustrous, strongly waved, prickle-margined leaves of great charm. In spring, the stem tips bear clusters of yellow flowers like tiny bells.

Rhododendron x
'Pink Pearl'. This vintage hybrid (circa 1890) is still one of the best for a shady site, producing annually huge trusses of large rose-pink flowers which slowly age lilac-pink and white. Eventually a tall evergreen shrub, it is inclined to get bare at the base.

Skimmia japonica

Erica cinerea 'Purple Beauty'

Skimmia japonica.
Happy in sun or shade, provided the soil stays reasonably moist, this is a most desirable small evergreen shrub of dome-like habit. Good glossy, evergreen leaves form a perfect background for trusses of fragrant white flowers and crimson berries. Male and female plants must be grown together however. Suggested are: 'Fragrans' (a free-blooming male) and 'Foremanii' (female). The recent cultivar 'Nymans' is said to be hermaphrodite.

SHRUBS FOR DRY SOILS

Ceanothus thyrsiflorus
'Repens'. This prostrate to dwarf evergreen has glossy, oval leaves and in late spring trusses of tiny pale blue flowers. An excellent shrub for clothing sunny banks.

Cytisus x beanii.
Raised as a chance hybrid at Kew Gardens in 1900. This is perhaps the best dwarf broom for the larger rock garden or sunny dry bank. Leafless green twigs become completely smothered with bright yellow pea flowers in late spring.

Erica cinerea.
Better known as bell heather, this variable prostrate to dwarf

evergreen shrub is a mainstay of the summer heather garden. There are cultivars in shades of purple, red, pink and white, all very free-flowering.

Helianthemum nummularium.
The common rock rose is a prostrate evergreen shrublet with satiny flowers, rather like tiny single roses, in shades of red, pink, yellow and white. Those with grey leaves are especially desirable; for example 'The Bride' (pink), 'Ben Hope' (carmine and orange) and 'Wisley White'.

Helianthemum 'The Bride'

Ruta graveolens.
Common rue or herb of grace is an acridly aromatic shrublet found in many herb gardens. It is also very decorative, having dissected blue-green leaves and mustard-yellow flower clusters.

SHRUBS FOR MOIST SOILS

Aronia arbutifolia.
This is the red chokeberry of
E.N.American swamps and moist
ground. A deciduous, medium sized
shrub, it has white flowers in spring,
red fruits in late summer and
brilliantly coloured foliage in
autumn.

Neillia thibetica.
Often listed as *N.longiracemosa*,
this suckering, medium to large
deciduous species deserves to be
grown more often. It has pleasing,
oval, sharply toothed and pointed
veiny leaves, and long, almost
catkin-like flower spikes of tiny
bright pink flowers.

Neillia thibetica

Salix caprea.
Sallow or goat willow is native to the
British Isles but still worthy of a
place in the larger garden. It has
apple-like foliage, greyish beneath,
usually turning yellow in autumn.
In early spring, the silvery male
catkins (pussy willow) expand and
finally turn yellow with pollen. *S.c.*
'Pendula', the Kilmarnock willow, is
a neat, small, grafted weeping
"tree".

Spiraea x billiardii
'Triumphans'. Listed in some
catalogues as *S.menziesii
triumphans*, this is a large,
suckering, deciduous shrub with
pale green oblong leaves. In
summer, every stem tip terminates
in a dense, plume-like cluster of
tiny, purple-rose flowers.

Viburnum opulus.
The guelder rose is also a native to
wet ground, but marvellously
adaptable to all kinds of soil. Its
white flower clusters, like those of a
lacecap hydrangea, are followed by
translucent red berries. In autumn
the leaves turn red, orange and
yellow. *V.o.* 'Sterile', the snowball
bush has ball-like clusters of sterile
flowers.

SHRUBS FOR LIMY SOILS

Fuchsia magellanica.
This hardy deciduous fuchsia
survives all but the coldest winters
outside though it is often cut back to
ground level. It does in fact, respond
to being cut down each late spring,
throwing up strong branched stems
to 1.2m (4ft) or so, clad with bright
green leaves and pendent red and
purple flowers. *F.m.* 'Gracilis' and
the white pink-tinted 'Molinae'
('Alba') are the hardiest. All fuchsias
thrive in limy soils.

Hebe x
'Carl Teschner'. Low hummock to
mat-forming, this little evergreen
shrublet is ideal for the rock garden
or front of the border. Tiny, dark,
evergreen leaves on almost black
stems make a good foil for the
profusely carried violet flowers.

Paeonia lutea ludlowii.
This is the largest flowered form of
the wild yellow tree peony. It is a
medium, sometimes almost large
deciduous shrub with big, fresh
green dissected leaves and clusters
of cup-shaped yellow flowers in early
summer.

Paeonia lutea ludlowii

Philadelphus x purpureomaculatus.
Cultivars of this hybrid are
distinguished by the fragrant cup-
shaped white flowers with a basal
purple flush. They are typified by
'Sybille', a small, deciduous shrub of
arching habit with freely produced
flowers. 'Belle Etoile' is more
compact and somewhat taller.

Weigela florida.
Sometimes still listed under
Diervilla, this is one of the most
popular early summer shrubs.
Mainly medium sized, but getting
large if not pruned, they come in
shades of pink, red and white.
'Newport Red' is the best crimson
and 'Fleur de Mai' the earliest pink.
'Foliis Purpureis' is a dwarf cultivar
with purple leaves and purple-pink
flowers.

SHRUBS FOR THE SEASIDE

Choisya ternata.
Although this medium sized shrub is
white flowered, it blooms so
abundantly and contrasts so well
with its own lustrous, deep
evergreen trifoliate leaves, it is
almost colourful.

Cytisus scoparius.
Common broom is well known for its
green leafless stems and profuse

yellow pea flowers. There are also
many different coloured cultivars,
notably 'Andreanus' (yellow and
crimson), 'Geoffrey Skipwith' (pink),
'Lord Lambourne' (crimson and
cream) and 'Our Princess' (mauve-
pink). All are medium sized.

Escallonia rubra.
Of medium to large size, this is one
of the best evergreen shrubs for the
seaside. The red flowers appear from
summer to late autumn. The semi-
evergreen hybrids are somewhat
smaller and more floriferous. All the
Donard cultivars are worth growing,
particularly 'Donard Beauty' (rich
rose-red), 'Donard Gem' (large pink)
and 'Donard Star' (rose-pink).

Escallonia 'Donard Star'

Genista lydia.
Rarely above 30cm (1ft) tall but
spreading to 1.2m (4ft) or even more,
this is perhaps the finest of the
dwarf brooms, becoming a solid
sheet of small yellow pea flowers in
early summer.

Viburnum tinus.
Perhaps better known as
laurustinus, this is a real seaside
gardener's standby; attractive
laurel-like evergreen foliage and
flat heads of white flowers,
sometimes from pink buds, in winter
and spring. The steely-blue berries
that follow are decidedly unusual.

Picture credits

John Glover: 1
Harry Smith Horticultural Photographic Collection: 4/5
All other pictures: Gillian Beckett

Artwork by Richard Prideaux & Steve Sandilands